My Husband, My Love

Copyright © 1997 Great Quotations, Inc.

All rights reserved. Written permission must be secured from the publisher to use or reproduce any part of this book, exept for brief quotations in critical reviews or articles.

Cover Design by Dmitry Feygin
Typography by Julie Otlewis

Published by Great Quotations
Publishing Co.,
Clendale Heights, IL

Library of Congress Catalog Card
Number: 96-078980

ISBN 1-56245-283-5

Printed in Hong Kong

To love a person means to agree to grow old with him.

— Albert Camus

How wonderful is that woman who continues to be a husband's sweetheart all her life.

For as many times as the waves embrace the shore is as many times as I think of you.

Some things in life are so special they are indescribable - that's how I feel about us.

— Gayle Lapekas

I hate being without you - because it's so easy to be with you.

— Gayle Lapekas

One of the best hearing aids a man can have is an attentive wife.

Take time to have fun with your loved one - remember, you can't cuddle up to money.

— Jack McElyea

*You are a part of me...
a part that I could
never live without.
And I hope that I never have to.*

L*ove is...*
*Wishing we'd
never quarreled.*

T*he best way to hold a man
is in your arms.*

— Mae West

I *need a hug from you -*
and only the way you can give it.

— Gayle Lapekas

H*appiness is:*
Someone to love.
Something to do and
Something to hope for.

Love is the master key that opens the gates of happiness.

— Oliver Wendell Holmes

*Treasure the love you receive above all.
It will survive long after your gold and good health
have vanished.*

— Og Mandino

The best and most beautiful things in the world cannot be seen, nor touched... but are felt in the heart.

— Helen Keller

Life is a flower of which love is the honey.

The heart is happiest when it beats for others.

We must resemble each other a little in order to understand each other, but we must be a little different to love each other.

— Paul Geraldy

*Don't walk in front of me,
I may not always follow...
Don't walk behind me,
I may not always lead...
Just walk beside me and
be my friend.*

N*ow abideth faith, hope, love, these three; but the greatest of these is Love.*

— Corinthians 13:13

Love is unselfish,
understanding and kind,
for it sees with its heart
and not with its mind.
Love is the answer that
everyone seeks.
Love is the language that
every heart speaks.
Love can't be bought,
it is priceless and free...
Love, like pure magic,
is a sweet mystery.

— Helen Steiner Rice

Nothing in life is as good as the marriage of true minds between man and woman. As good? It is life itself.

— Pearl Buck

A *successful marriage requires falling in love many times, always with the same person.*

— Mignon McLaughlin

A simple enough pleasure, surely, to have breakfast alone with one's husband, but how seldom married people in the midst of life achieve it.

— Anne Morrow Lindbergh

*Whatever our souls
are made of,
his and mine are the same.*

— Emily Bronte

Love is having somebody to nudge when you see something you like and want to share it.

*If I had never met him
I would have dreamed him
into being.*

— Anzia Yezierska

L ove is like the magic touch of stars.

— Walter Benton

H aving someone with whom to laugh, talk, cry and dream is having a friend to love.

Love is when each person is more concerned for the other than for one's self.

— David Frost

*Love, the magician,
knows this little trick
whereby two people
walk in different directions
yet always remain
side by side.*

— Hugh Prather

What is love...but a friend who has remained beside me and never once removed his hand.

— Hugh Prather

*To love is nothing.
To be loved is something.
To love, and be loved,
is everything.*

— T. Tolis V.

The best gifts are tied with heartstrings.

*L ove doesn't make the
world go 'round.
Love is what makes the
ride worthwhile.*

— Franklin P. Jones

Love does not consist of gazing at each other but in looking outward together in the same direction.

— Antoine de Saint-Exupery

...love from one being to another can only be that two solitudes come nearer, recognize and protect and comfort each other.

— Han Suyin

I love you, not because you're perfect,
but because you're so perfect for me.

Couples who love each other tell each other a thousand things without talking.

— Chinese Proverb

*Oh, the comfort, the
inexpressible comfort,
of feeling safe with a person,
having neither to weigh
thoughts nor measure words,
but pouring them all
right out, just as they are,
chaff and grain together;
certain that a faithful hand
will take and sift them,
keep what is worth keeping
and with a breath of
kindness blow the rest away.*

*Love understands love;
it needs no talk.*

— Francis Ridley Havergal

*It is comforting to know
each word or silence
is understood.*

*Love is friendship
caught on fire.
It is quiet understanding,
mutual confidence,
sharing and forgiving.
It is loyalty through good
and bad times.
It settles for less
than perfection, and makes
allowances for
human weaknesses.*

T*wo souls with but a single thought,*
Two hearts that beat as one.

— Von Munch Bellinghausen

The entire sum of existence is the magic of being needed by just one person.

— V. Putnam

*True love doesn't have a
happy ending;
true love doesn't have
an ending.*

I just wanted to let you know... how nice it feels inside when my smile is showing and my heart is full and my thoughts are all for you.

When we're not together...
I seem to spend my time
wishing that we were.

The one word that makes a
partnership successful
is 'OURS.'

Here I am again sitting alone,
daydreaming about you -
with dreams that leave
a smile in my heart.

*Is it fair that you occupy
so many of my thoughts -
and so much of my heart?*

— Gayle Lapekas

F*or I do love you...*
as the dew loves the flowers;
as the birds love the sunshine;
as the wavelets love the breeze.

— Mark Twain

*If I know what love is,
it is because of you.*

— Herman Hesse

There is only one thing for a man to do who is married to a woman who enjoys spending money and that is to enjoy earning it.

— Ed Howe

*In all hearts there is music.
If we listen carefully,
we can hear
each other's song.*

*Marriage should be a duet -
when one sings,
the other claps.*

— Joe Murray

Kissing is a means of getting two people so close together that they can't see anything wrong with each other.

— Rene Yasenek

Marriages are made
in heaven.

— John Lyly

As most veterans
will tell you,
marriage is the continuous
process of getting used
to things you hadn't expected.

A good marriage is that in which each appoints the other the guardian of his solitude.

— Rainier Maria Rilke

*To love is to admire
with the heart;
to admire is to
love with the mind.*

— Theophile Gautier

*Marriage is three parts love
and seven parts forgiveness
of sins.*

— Mitchell

Come live with me,
and be my Love;
And we will all
the pleasures prove.

— Christopher Marlowe

A man without a wife
is but half a man.

The great secret of a successful marriage is to treat all disasters as incidents and none of the incidents as disasters.

— Harold Nicholson

I wouldn't miss life with you...
for anything.

Love is sharing all of
the wonderful things life
has to offer with the person
you care most about.

A husband should tell his wife everything that he is sure she will find out, and before anyone else does.

— Thomas Robert Dewar

A *good wife and health are a man's best wealth.*

— Proverb

To love is to place our happiness in the happiness of another.

— G.W. Leibnitz

Anything is possible if you do it together!

Whoever loves much, does much.

— Thomas A. Kempis

*Where love is concerned,
too much is not ever enough.*

— Pierre-Augustin Caron De Beaumarchais

*Don't marry someone
you can live with.
Marry someone you
can't live without.*

Love is not a matter of counting the years; it's making the years count.

— William Smith

Any time that is not spent on love is wasted.

— Tasso

Love is being stupid together.

— Paul Valery

Before marriage the three little words are "I love you." After marriage they are "Let's eat out."